TESTI CANCER

The Essential Guide

Priya Shah

Testicular Cancer – The Essential Guide is also available in accessible formats for people with any degree of visual impairment. The large print edition and e-book (with accessibility features enabled) are available from Need2Know. Please let us know if there are any special features you require and we will do our best to accommodate your needs.

First published in Great Britain in 2012 by
Need2Know
Remus House
Coltsfoot Drive
Peterborough
PE2 9BF
Telephone 01733 898103
Fax 01733 313524
www.need2knowbooks.co.uk

Contents

Introduction 5

Chapter 1   What is Testicular Cancer? 7

Chapter 2   Symptoms and Warning Signs 17

Chapter 3   Obtaining Medical Advice 23

Chapter 4   Understanding Your Diagnosis 31

Chapter 5   Treatment Options 39

Chapter 6   General Coping and Support Advice 51

Chapter 7   Prognosis Overview 59

Chapter 8   Surveillance and Aftercare 65

Chapter 9   Lowering the Risks of Cancer 73

Glossary   79

Help List   83

Introduction

This book is dedicated to all men, and their loved ones, desiring to learn more about testicular cancer. Whether you have been diagnosed with testicular cancer, know someone with the condition or simply want to learn more about this type of cancer, the information in this volume will help you better understand the causes, types of cancer, treatments and any prevention tips related to testicular cancer.

Testicular cancer is, unfortunately, a very common health condition affecting men from all over the world. However, it is also the most curable cancer and patients usually have very good chances of fighting back and surviving it. However, no matter how good the survival rates are, it is certainly understandable that you may feel overwhelmed, lonely or even in distress if you are at risk of or have been diagnosed with testicular cancer. It is for this exact reason that this book has been developed; each chapter will communicate valuable information on testicular cancer, on top of walking you through each step, from your initial consultation with your physician to going back to normal after chemotherapy and radiation therapy.

Annexed to this book you will also find a comprehensive list of support groups and helplines that can provide you with additional information and help should you be diagnosed with testicular cancer or live with a cancer patient.

Disclaimer

All the information compiled within this sensitive and informative guide has been taken from reliable medical websites and cancer resources. However, the advice given in here should not be taken as a substitute for a doctor's advice, and it is highly encouraged to schedule an appointment with a health professional should you develop any symptoms or have any further questions after reading the information detailed in this book.

Chapter One

What is Testicular Cancer?

Before we get to that, let's see what the testicles are and what exactly their function in the male body is.

Testicles (singular) or testes (plural) are male organs that produce sperm, and are the most important part of the male reproductive system. Their female counterparts are the ovaries.

Where are they located?

They are situated in a sac underneath the penis, called the scrotum. The scrotum keeps the testes outside the body so that they can be maintained at three degrees Fahrenheit less than body temperature. This is vital for sperm production.

What is their function?

The primary function of the testes is to produce sperm, other than this, they also produce the male hormone called testosterone. It is this hormone that turns a boy into an adult at the time of puberty. The changes that take place are the production of sperm, elongation and thickening of the penis, growth of hairs in different parts of the body, like the face, armpits and the pubic region. The other changes seen are deepening of the voice and a secondary bout of growth. The secondary bout of growth includes increase in height, increase in bone density, and increased musculature of the body. Inside each testes there

'The primary function of the testes is to produce sperm and the hormone testosterone.'

are two types of cells. They are the Sertoli cells and the Leydig cells. The Sertoli cells produce sperm and the Leydig cells produce the male hormone testosterone.

So, what is testicular cancer?

You might know that cancer is the uncontrolled proliferation of cells in the body, and testicular cancer is no different. In testicular cancer, there is abnormal proliferation of cells inside the testicle. Although testicular cancer can be derived from any cell type present in the testicle, more than 95% of cases are derived from germ cells, which are sperm-producing cells of the testes. The remaining 5% are sex cord-gonadal stromal tumour.

Germ cell tumour of the testicles can be broadly divided into two main groups which are further divided into different subgroups. They are:

'The incidence of testicular cancer has risen to 1.2% per year.'

Seminoma

※ Classic type.

※ Anaplastic type.

※ Spermatocytic type.

Non-seminoma

※ Choriocarcinoma.

※ Embryonal carcinoma.

※ Teratoma

※ Yolk sac tumours.

The seminoma type of testicular cancer is the most curable and easily treatable form. The survival rate of patients diagnosed with seminoma type cancer is more than 95%, and the prognosis is excellent. Even though treatment might require removal of one testicle, this does not affect fertility or sexual functions. About half of the germ cell tumours of the testicle are the seminoma type.

The non-seminoma group of testicular cancer has a lower cure rate of 70 to 95%.

- Choriocarcinoma type is an aggressive, malignant type of cancer. It is characterized by early spread to the lungs via the blood route.

- Embryonal carcinoma is an uncommon variety of testicular cancer. Average age of onset of this variety of cancer is 31 years. This cancer type also has a high chance of spreading to other organs in the body.

- Teratomas are tumours with a capsule around them. Because of the presence of the capsule around them, teratomas are usually benign, although malignant forms are also seen, but very rare. This tumour is formed of tissues not normally found at the site of formation of the tumour. They can contain teeth, bones, hair, and even more complex organs like eyes, feet, hands etc. Teratomas are thought to occur in the body at the time of birth.

- Yolk sac tumour is the most common testicular tumour in children under three years of age. It is quite a rare type. This age group also has good prognosis.

The differentiation of different type of testicular cancer is done by a pathologist after collecting tissue samples from the testicle. It is very important to identify the subtype of testicular cancer, as the treatment options and the prognosis of different types vary.

'Non-seminoma group of testicular cancer has a lower cure rate of 70 to 95%.'

The current picture

Testicular cancer is the most common type of cancer in the age group of 15 to 34 years.

Males over the age of 50 years also have slightly more chance of developing this cancer as compared to the normal population. Males below 20 years are at risk if they had undescended testicles which was diagnosed late.

Compared with other types of cancer, testicular cancer is very rare. But in the last two decades the number of reported cases of testicular cancer is on the rise. The incidence of testicular cancer has risen to 1.2% per year. Statistics say, that in the US almost 8,000 cases of testicular cancer are reported every year, and in UK approximately 2,000 cases are registered. It is estimated that approximately 400 deaths a year occur in the US due to testicular cancer. This cancer is more common in white men than African-American or other races. Scandinavia and New Zealand have higher incidence rates than other countries.

The only positive thing about testicular cancer is that it has one of the highest cure rates among all cancer types. It is easier to be cured completely if detected at an early stage. This is because at this stage, the tumour will only be confined to the inside of the scrotum. Even for relatively few cases where it has spread outside the testes, the cure rate is over 80%. This is very encouraging, and is due to the fact that testicular cancers are very sensitive to chemotherapy. So even at this late stage they can be cured completely. The risk of dying from testicular cancer is very low, about 1 in 5,000 cases.

'Testicular cancer has one of the highest cure rates among all cancer types.'

'I am afraid. I'm suffering from testicular cancer'. This is a statement that many people are shy to say to their loved ones. This is mainly due to the social stigma associated with it, because the testes and the hormones they produce are considered as the signs of masculinity. But if you are feeling stigmatised or discriminated by your friends or at your workplace, you will find it helpful to speak to others who may be experiencing or have experienced similar problems in their lives. One very helpful thing that you can do is to contact a local support group for testicular cancer. Make sure you attend them at least once a month. You will find that being able to receive and give support to others, will benefit you immensely. See the help list for more information.

What causes testicular cancer?

Nobody really knows. That would be the simplest answer. But during the past decade, researchers have learned a great deal about the reason for the development of testicular cancer. But they have not been able to pinpoint the exact cause.

Our current understanding of the aetiology of the disease, says that the disease is linked with a number of other conditions, which are described in detail in the following section. Apart from this, genetics plays a big role in the development of testicular cancer. Scientists have found that certain changes in the chromosomes and DNA may cause normal cells in the testicle(s) to develop into tumours called germ cell tumours. Chromosomes are long strands of DNA that carry genetic information about inherited traits of humans. Each sperm from the male, and the egg from the female has half the number of chromosome (23) of a complete human cell. So, when the sperm and egg combine they result in the formation of a complete human cell with 46 chromosomes. This is why we tend to inherit traits and looks from both of our parents.

So, how does this 46-chromosome cell change to cells with half the number of chromosomes (23) in the first place? This process happens inside the testicles and is known as meiosis. A testicular tumour (germ cell type) develops when something untoward happens to this process. As a result, abnormal cells will retain all the 46 chromosomes. These chromosomes become unstable over time and progressively become more abnormal in their size and number, and develop into a germ cell tumour. Scientists are studying these chromosomes to learn more about what exactly goes wrong during meiosis, and to find the true cause of testicular cancer.

Risk factors for developing testicular cancer

Scientists have found a few risk factors that make a man more prone to developing testicular cancer. They are:

▪ Undescended testicle(s) – One of the main risk factors for developing testicular cancer is undescended testicle(s) or medically called 'cryptorchidism'.

In a normally growing foetus, the testicles grow inside the abdomen of the foetus, and they move (descend) into the scrotum before birth. But in 3% of boys, the testicles do not descend into the scrotum before birth. In some cases the testicles remain inside the abdomen, while in other cases they will be stuck somewhere on the way down into the scrotum. Most of the time, during the first year of life, the stuck testicles will slowly move down into the scrotum. And if the testicles have not reached the scrotum by the time the child turns two years, they probably won't go down on their own. In this case, they or it have to be surgically placed in the scrotum. This surgical procedure is known as 'orchiopexy'.

The risk of developing testicular cancer is higher in men whose testicles had stayed in the abdomen after birth, opposed to those that had descended at least partway. It is seen that three out of four cases of testicular cancer develop in individuals who had a history of undescended testicles.

If the child has undergone orchiopexy, it is likely to reduce the chance of developing testicular cancer. But, the best time to undergo the surgery is still not clear.

'Only 3% of cases of testicular cancer are found to occur in males with family history.'

- Family history – Like any other type of cancer, the risk of developing testicular cancer is higher in individuals with a family history of the disease. If a man has the disease, the risk of developing testicular cancer is higher in one or more of his brothers or sons. But this is not such a significant risk factor, as statistics show that only 3% of cases of testicular cancer are found to occur in males with family history.

- Carcinoma in situ (CIS) – This is an early form of cancer stage, where no cancer cells are found in the surrounding tissue, and there is no mass or any symptoms of a cancer. It has been found that in some percentages of people having carcinoma in situ of the testicles, after some time they progress to full-blown testicular cancer. CIS is found more in men who have undergone testicular biopsy as part of their infertility evaluation and treatment, or in men who have undergone surgery to remove a testicle because of cryptorchidism. But this doesn't mean that people with CIS should be treated as cancer patients. The best recommended approach is to wait and see if CIS becomes worse or turns into true cancer, because treatment of CIS with chemotherapy and radiotherapy has its own risks and side effects, and not all cases of CIS turn into full-blown cancer. So, the risk of treating CIS far outweighs the benefit.

- HIV infection – Some evidence points to the fact that men who are infected with HIV, particularly those men who have developed AIDS, are at a higher risk of developing testicular cancer.

- Age – 90% of cases of testicular cancer occur in the age group of 15 to 54. Men between 15 to 35 years of age are at the highest risk. This cancer plagues men at a time when health issues are the last thing on their mind. They are usually thinking about starting a family or getting a job. But being diagnosed with testicular cancer is not the end of the world. You don't have to look far to find great personalities who have conquered the disease and are living a normal and productive life. One such example is that of Lance Edward Armstrong who is an American former professional cyclist, and who has won the prestigious Tour de France a record seven consecutive times after having survived testicular cancer.

- Race and ethnicity – The risk of testicular cancer is highest among white men. The risk is almost five times greater than that of black men and three times that of Asian-American or American-Indian men. In short, the worldwide risk of testicular cancer is highest among men living in Europe and America and lowest in Asia and Africa.

- Congenital abnormality – It is seen that there is slightly higher risk in men with congenital abnormality of the penis, kidney and testicles, as well as men with a history of inguinal hernia.

- Body size – Some studies have found that testicular cancer is more prevalent in taller men, while other studies have not. So this risk factor is inconclusive.

Other unproven risk factors

It is a myth that horseback riding or prior trauma to the testicles increases the chance of developing testicular cancer. There is no scientific evidence to prove this.

Most studies also have not found any link between strenuous physical activity and testicular cancer. Being physically active will only reduce your chances of getting any form of cancer.

Does this mean that I will develop testicular cancer if I have one or more risk factors?

No, having one or more risk factors doesn't mean you will develop testicular cancer in the near future. It just means that a man with a risk factor has slightly more chance over the normal population of developing testicular cancer.

Summing Up

- The testicle (singular) or testes (plural) are the male organs that produce sperm, and the most important part of the male reproductive system.

- The primary function of the testicles is to produce sperm and the hormone testosterone.

- Based on the cells in the tumour, testicular cancer can be broadly divided into two main groups, seminoma and non-seminoma types.

- The seminoma types of testicular cancer are the most curable and easily treatable forms of testicular cancer. The survival rate of patients diagnosed with any one of them is more than 95%, and the prognosis is excellent.

- The non-seminoma group of testicular cancer has a lower cure rate of 70 to 95%.

- Testicular cancer is the most common type of cancer in the age group of 15 to 34 years.

- The risk of dying from testicular cancer is very low, about 1 in 5,000 cases.

- Certain changes in the chromosomes and DNA may cause normal cells in the testicles to develop into tumours called germ cell tumours.

- There are a number of risk factors for developing testicular cancer including: a history of having undescended testicle(s), family history and age. Having any one of these risk factors does not automatically mean a man will develop the disease.

Chapter Two

Symptoms and Warning Signs

Similar to most health conditions, testicular cancer can be diagnosed early if symptoms are noticed. Knowing what to look for and what indicates that something might not be normal is the first step in diagnosing testicular cancer. Let's look at the various signs and symptoms associated with this condition, as well as how you can conduct your very own self-exam. Self-examination is known to be one of the main reasons testicular cancer gets diagnosed early, which can greatly improve the outcome of your condition.

What are the most common symptoms of testicular cancer?

The easiest way to diagnose testicular cancer is to execute regular self-exams, which you will learn more about shortly. But how do you know what to look for? Testicular cancer can present a few different signs and symptoms; here is a list of the most common symptoms associated with the disease:

- Lumps.
- Pain.
- Swelling.

These are perhaps the three symptoms most commonly associated with this particular cancer. Should you notice any of these symptoms, it would be very wise to get in touch with your doctor immediately. While these may or may not indicate testicular cancer, they are certainly a sign that something is wrong and needs to be checked out by a health professional. However, it is possible that you may exhibit other symptoms than those listed previously.

Some men eventually diagnosed with testicular cancer have complained of an aching feeling in the lower abdomen (as opposed to the testicles themselves), a feeling of heaviness in the scrotum, general discomfort in the testicular area and loss of sex drive. In rare cases, patients may experience breast tenderness or swelling.

It can never be repeated enough that the earlier a diagnosis is made, the better your chances of healing and fighting the cancer will be. If you feel that something is abnormal, wrong or unusual, do not hesitate to request a consultation with a doctor. An initial consultation with a health professional will help determine whether further tests are necessary to confirm diagnosis or if your symptoms are caused by a different condition altogether. Either way, anything abnormal should be reported to your GP.

'It is recommended to get a medical exam as soon as any type of symptom is noticed.'

Symptoms related to advanced cancer

It may happen that certain cancer patients experience no symptoms at all at first. This would cause the cancer to go undetected for a while, which gives it the opportunity to spread to other parts of the body. A cancer that has spread throughout the human body is referred to as an 'advanced cancer' (metastasis). However, it is also said that only about 1 man out of 4 experiences any symptoms from advanced cancer.

Testicular cancer can easily spread to the retroperitoneal lymph nodes, due to their proximity to the genital area. This will cause you to experience lower back or belly pain.

If the cancer has spread to the lungs, patients will experience shortness of breath, chest pains and coughing, amongst other symptoms.

If you experience confusion or headaches, it might be a sign that the cancer has spread to your brain – which, fortunately, only happens in rare cases.

Different symptoms for different types of cancer

We've already explored the idea that there are different types of testicular cancer. Below you'll find more precise information as to which symptoms relate to which particular type of cancer.

Germ cell tumours

Germ cell tumours are usually easy to diagnose as they present themselves with a lump on the testicle. This particular type of tumour might also raise the levels of hCG (human chorionic gonadotropin), a hormone that may make a man's breast grow or become tender.

Stromal tumour

While the stromal tumour is much less common than its counterpart, it still causes very particular symptoms. Estrogen-producing tumours will be associated with a loss of sex drive and enlarged breasts. Androgen-producing tumours, on the other hand, usually do not present any symptoms in grown men. In the eventuality of a young boy developing an androgen-producing testicular tumour, the patient will observe growth of facial and body hair at a much younger age than normal.

How can I conduct my own testicular self-exam?

More often than not, diagnosis of testicular cancer starts with a self-exam. Doctors recommend that all boys and men over the age of 14 practise a testicular self-examination (TSE) each month. This not only allows them to make sure that they are in good health, but also allows them to get a diagnosis and treatment plan quickly and early on should any abnormalities be detected. Practising monthly testicular self-examinations will also help you understand your body and gain a better understanding of how everything feels and looks when normal, so that you are better equipped to notice any changes or suspicious symptoms.

The first step in the testicular self-examination is to stand in front of a mirror without clothing. You'll want to make sure that you have good lighting and that nothing can obstruct your view as you perform the examination. Since you'll be looking for abnormalities, it is of the utmost importance that you can see clearly from all angles.

- Start by looking for any swelling in the scrotum area. This should be rather easy to spot in the eventuality that there is swelling.

- Then, place the index and middle fingers under your testicles and roll them gently between your fingers.

- Behind the testicles, you'll find the epididymis, which resembles a soft tube.

If everything is normal, which means that you didn't see any swelling or find any lumps or anything else suspicious, take a breath and relax.

However, if you think you may have found something that needs to be checked out, do not hesitate to do so. While a lump or any other suspicious-looking characteristic may not necessarily signify that you have testicular cancer, it is better to be safe than sorry.

'It is recommended to perform the testicular self-examination after a warm shower or bath, as this relaxes the scrotum.'

Summing Up

- The three most common symptoms associated with testicular cancer are lumps, pain and swelling in the testicular area.

- Other less common symptoms include lower abdomen pain, heaviness in the scrotum, loss of sex drive and tenderness in the breasts.

- Advanced stages of testicular cancer may spread to the lymph nodes, lungs and brain.

- Symptoms associated with advanced testicular cancer include lower back pain, shortness of breath and headaches.

- Germ cell tumours will often present themselves with a lump, while stromal tumours affect the hormone levels.

- Testicular self-examination, or TSE, is one of the most efficient methods leading to early diagnosis of testicular cancer.

- TSE should be performed once a month for all boys and men over the age of 14. You should be looking for lumps, swelling or any other abnormalities that you may not have noticed before. Always consult a doctor if you find anything abnormal.

Chapter Three

Obtaining Medical Advice

When should I consult a doctor?

It is very important to emphasise that anything abnormal needs to be examined by a doctor. Whether it is related to cancer or not, in the end you must make sure that your body is in good health and anything different or suspicious should be checked out. You must absolutely contact your GP if you notice a lump or hardness in one of your testicles, an unexplained enlargement of your testicles or any pain or swelling in the genital area.

Certain individuals are more at risk of testicular cancer than others, and these individuals should be even more careful when performing self-examination. If you have undescended testes, previous history of testicular tumour (yourself or family) or are infertile, you must be especially vigilant. However, self-examinations are highly recommended for every man, not only the ones falling within the various risk factors aforementioned.

Of course, it may happen that an abnormality detected by the patient turns out to be related to an entirely different condition than testicular cancer, such as epididymal cysts, torsion of the testicle and hydrocele, for example. However, these conditions all need to be examined by a doctor, and a consultation can certainly put your mind at ease if you are experiencing any of the previously mentioned symptoms.

The importance of visiting the doctor

Let's face it, there is a certain stigma associated with testicular cancer, if not cancer in general. You may feel ashamed of having something 'abnormal' or even scared of the possibility of having cancer in the groin area – if nowhere else. Many individuals skip over essential self-examinations, do not pay attention to warning signs or simply delay consulting their doctor in the case of abnormalities. It will never be stressed enough that testicular cancer diagnosed early has higher cure rates. If you suspect that something may be wrong or present higher risks of testicular cancer than other men, you absolutely must consult your doctor. Self-examinations are a great way to help for early diagnosis of testicular cancer but if you are not a doctor yourself, you might miss something or overlook a small bump because it doesn't look so bad... yet.

On the other hand, you might feel embarrassed by the idea of dropping your pants in front of a stranger, or fear that you are wasting your doctor's time by asking him or her to check something that might be benign. No matter what your reason is for not seeking medical advice, it isn't a good reason. While many men simply ignore a lump and hope for it to go away, this isn't the right approach and could end up changing your entire life, should the lump turn out to be a tumour. You can also be assured that your doctor has seen it all, has seen worse and that you're not the first patient to come in for a consultation. Put your shame aside and do yourself a favour that could save your life. Doctors are professionals and should make you feel comfortable even in the most awkward or uncomfortable situation.

'No matter what your reason is for not seeking medical advice, it isn't a good reason.'

The bottom line is, if you notice something abnormal in your testicular area, schedule an appointment with your GP. During your appointment, your doctor will perform an examination and will ask you a few questions about your health. If there is any chance at all that a lump or other symptom may be related to testicular cancer, you will be asked to undergo additional tests or you will be referred to a specialist, such as oncologist, for example.

What questions should I ask my doctor prior to diagnosis?

One mistake that many men do is to not ask the right questions. If you're at the doctor's office because you've found a lump on your testicles, chances are that your mind is racing and that hundreds of scenarios are running through your head. The best advice that can be given to anyone consulting a doctor for a lump or any abnormality is to stay calm and ask questions.

Your doctor is used to this kind of situation; they've probably had many other individuals sitting in their office, expecting the worst. Breathe deeply and relax. You've already made the first step in the right direction by consulting a health professional. Armed with the right information, you'll have a better idea of what to expect and how to handle the situation. Here is a list of questions that you should ask your doctor prior to any testing:

- What exactly is it that you are looking for?
- How can these tests help you form a diagnosis?
- How accurate are the results of these tests?
- When will the results be ready?
- Are the tests given here or do I have to go to a different location?
- Will there be any pain involved with these tests?

Of course, feel free to add any of your own personal questions to this list. The goal is to make sure that you know what to expect from here on and trust your doctor at each step of the way. It is highly recommended to write your questions down and take a list to your appointment. This way, you won't forget anything even if you are nervous or startled, and will be sure to have all the information in hand to move forward in the process. After all, we are discussing your health and the eventuality that you may or may not have cancer. Asking questions is essential.

How is testicular cancer diagnosed?

First off, if you exhibit any signs or symptoms, your doctor will take a complete medical history to see if you are at risk and have experienced other symptoms that you may not have noticed. Your entire family history may also be explored, so be prepared to answer questions related to your close family – you may want to find out if any close relatives have a history of testicular cancer or any other major conditions prior to visiting your doctor. He or she will also feel your testicles to look for swelling, tenderness or lumps, before examining your abdomen, lymph nodes, or any other part of your body that could be affected by the spreading of testicular cancer.

In certain cases, it is possible that your doctor requires more specialised tests. These can be ordered even if nothing abnormal was found through a physical exam, so there is no need to be concerned before the results are in. Testing can be used to help establish a diagnosis, but also to help establish the best treatment plan should you be diagnosed with testicular cancer. There is quite a wide variety of tests that can be used to diagnose cancer and the choice of test will be made according to your age and medical condition, the type of cancer suspected, the severity of symptoms and any previous test results obtained. After the initial physical examination, your doctor may order any of the following:

Ultrasounds

If you or your doctor find a lump on your testicles, an ultrasound will help determine the nature of that lump. Ultrasounds are used to confirm whether the lump is solid or filled with fluid. The ultrasound will also help determine whether further tests are needed to confirm a diagnosis. This is usually one of the best methods to diagnose cancer. If your doctor does not recommend the use of ultrasounds, make sure to ask him or her what the reason is so that you are aware of what pushed this decision. While there may be a good reason for bypassing the ultrasound, you still want to make sure that nothing is being overlooked and that you understand why your doctor has chosen a different method for your diagnosis.

> 'Testing can be used to help establish a diagnosis, but also to help establish the best treatment plan should you be diagnosed with testicular cancer.'

Biopsy

The doctor may also order a biopsy to help confirm a cancer diagnosis. During a biopsy, a portion of tissue will be removed from the scrotum and sent to a laboratory for further investigation. At this time, a biopsy is rarely used to diagnose testicular cancer; if cancer is suspected, the standard procedure is usually to remove the entire testicle. However, a biopsy of the lungs or other parts of the body can be used if it is suspected that the cancer has spread to various organs throughout the body.

Blood tests

These tests are used to detect higher than normal levels of certain substances in your blood. If you are a cancer patient, substances such as AFP (alpha-fetoprotein), LDH (lactate dehydrogenase) and hCG (human chorionic gonadtropin) are found in higher concentration than usual in your blood, acting as tumour markers. Even if your physical exam did not hint to any symptoms or signs of testicular cancer, even a slight change in the levels of these substances could indicate that further investigation is needed. Blood tests may also be required along with urine tests.

Imaging

Another way to detect testicular cancer is to use body images. These can be obtained through X-rays and scans. The different types of imaging used to diagnose cancer are:

- X-rays – This type of imaging creates a picture of the inside of your body using radiation. It may be that your doctor recommends a chest X-ray to determine if the cancer has spread to your lungs.

- CT scan – This is used to create a three-dimensional image of the inside of your body. CT scans are used to evaluate the abdomen, pelvis, chest, brain and any other areas recommended by your doctor.

- MRI – These act similarly to CT scans, by providing a three-dimensional view of the inside of the body. However, these are rarely used for testicular cancer diagnosis, unless the physical examination indicates that the cancer may have spread to the brain.

Cancer stages

Once these tests have been conducted and the results are in, the doctor will most likely be able to establish a diagnosis. If a cancer diagnosis is established, the next step will be to stage the cancer. Testicular cancer usually presents itself in three different stages:

- Stage I indicates that the disease is present and confined in the testicle and spermatic cord.

- Stage II indicates that the disease has spread to the abdominal lymph nodes.

- Stage III indicates that the disease has spread to organs or lymph nodes located outside the abdominal region.

More information will be given about the various stages of testicular cancer in the following chapter.

What's next?

At this point you have noticed an abnormality, consulted a doctor and submitted yourself to various tests to help establish a diagnosis. What's next?

'If a cancer diagnosis is established, the next step will be to stage the cancer.'

If your doctor has yet to do so, he or she will discuss the diagnosis with you. It is very important to openly communicate with your doctor, as you will need to make informed decisions about your health, treatment plan, etc. You had questions prior to undergoing any testing, and you most likely have even more questions now that a diagnosis has been made. Here is a list of questions that you should ask your doctor once a cancer diagnosis has been established.

- Are other tests needed or recommended to confirm my diagnosis?

- What stage is my cancer?

- What are the treatment options recommended for my type of cancer?

- Are there any clinical trials currently available for testicular cancer patients?

- Who will be coordinating my treatment?

- Are there any possible side effects for each treatment option?

- Will those treatments limit my daily activities?

- Should I discuss with a fertility specialist prior to starting treatment?

- What are the chances that the cancer comes back after treatment?

- Will there be any follow-up testing needed?

- How much will this cost, and who can help me with financial details?

- Is the treatment plan recommended the standard treatment for my type of cancer?

- Are there any support groups or organisations who I can get in touch with?

You must make sure that you are fully aware of the implications of your diagnosis and the treatment plan established by your doctor. Asking questions is the only way for you to build trust with your health-care team and ensure that you have full disclosure on everything related to your treatment. You will also have to sign consent forms at the doctor's office and you should only sign them if you are fully aware of all the implications and have been given full disclosure on the treatments you are about to receive.

On the other hand, if you have received the wonderful news that you do not have testicular cancer, make sure to ask your doctor what caused your symptoms and if you should follow-up in order to monitor the situation.

'You must make sure that you are fully aware of the implications of your diagnosis and the treatment plan established by your doctor.'

Summing Up

▨ You should consult your doctor if you notice anything abnormal in the scrotum area.

▨ While your symptoms may be associated with a different condition, only a health professional can make a diagnosis and you should not rely on a book, the Internet or the advice of your friends or family to jump to conclusions.

▨ You should not feel embarrassed or anxious to consult a doctor; delaying a consultation is not recommended if you exhibit any symptoms.

▨ Always ask questions prior to undergoing any testing – take a list of questions to your initial consultation to make sure that you get all the answers you need to move forward.

▨ There are various ways to pose a testicular cancer diagnosis. The testing options offered to you will be based on your age, medical condition, type of cancer suspected, severity of symptoms and any previous test results obtained.

▨ Ultrasounds are the most common testing option to be used for testicular cancer.

▨ Other tests ordered by your doctor may include a biopsy, blood and urine tests and various imaging scans and X-rays.

▨ Testicular cancer is generally classified in three stages, indicating whether the cancer is localised or has spread to other regions and areas of the body.

▨ Make sure to discuss your diagnosis with your doctor. Similar to your initial consultation, make sure to ask questions and get clear answers when it comes to your treatment plan, as you will be asked to make decisions later on. The patient's informed consent is necessary in the medical profession.

Chapter Four

Understanding Your Diagnosis

It is very important to understand your diagnosis; many individuals listen to their doctor without asking questions, or understanding how the doctor came to a particular diagnosis, or what it entails. If you are faced with the possibility of testicular cancer, it is necessary for you to learn more about differential diagnosis, staging and more. While some of these topics have been previously explored, it is important to dig deeper within the information already provided in order to really have a good understanding of testicular cancer so that you can be better prepared for what is to come.

What is differential diagnosis?

In short, a differential diagnosis is a diagnosis that explores all of the possible causes of certain symptoms. For example, nasal congestion can signify a simple cold but can also be a symptom of a sinusitis. Using a differential diagnosis is a great way to make sure that the final diagnosis is the right one, as all the other options and possibilities will be explored and eliminated to find the most accurate explanation for a set of symptoms. There are even doctors, often referred to as diagnosticians, who specialise in differential diagnosis.

The first step in performing a differential diagnosis is for the doctor to do a thorough review of the patient's case. In the case that you are the patient, the doctor will ask you a variety of questions about your symptoms, your health history and if there is a family history of certain diseases. Of course, you'll also be subjected to a series of tests to support hypotheses and theories related to your condition. The information collected through questioning and testing will then be assessed by your doctor in order to come up with a final diagnosis

'A differential diagnosis is a diagnosis that explores all of the possible causes of certain symptoms.'

that may or may not include multiple causes for your symptoms. It is only after a final diagnosis has been established that treatment can begin; the final diagnosis will establish with a higher level of certainty what is causing your symptoms, which in turn establishes how you will be treated and which medication or drug will be used to minimise symptoms.

Differential diagnosis often depends on how accurate and honest you are in reporting your symptoms. This is why it is very important – especially in the case of testicular cancer, which is a rather sensitive issue for many – to be completely open with your doctor and report all your symptoms, no matter how uncomfortable it may be. A small omission can make an incredible difference and may even lead to fatal mistake. Make sure to discuss every symptom, every concern, every abnormality – whether it seems important or not, or related to testicular cancer or not.

'Make sure to discuss every symptom, every concern, every abnormality – whether it seems important or not, or related to testicular cancer or not.'

Some common differentials related to testicular cancer

Because symptoms associated with testicular cancer can also easily be associated with other conditions of the genital area, it is very important to understand the implication of differential diagnosis. Enlargement of the testicles, pain, swelling, heaviness and many other symptoms can easily be signs of something other than cancer. Following is a list of other conditions that can be included in the process of a differential diagnosis for testicular cancer. Please note that this list is not exhaustive and other conditions can also be included in a differential diagnosis.

Benign tumour

A benign tumour is non-cancerous. While it still presents itself under the form of an abnormal mass of tissue in a localised area, it can be easily removed and does not cause extensive damage to the human body, as opposed to malignant tumours. Many individuals who notice a bump or lump on their testicles will jump to conclusions and expect the worst; however there is still a chance that the lump is a benign tumour – a simple test can determine whether the lump is a malignant or non-malignant tumour.

Epididymitis

Epididymitis is an inflammation of the epididymis, a small tube connecting the testicles with the vas deferens (the tube that connects the testes with the urethra). It is often found in men between 19 and 35 years of age and often results from an infection of the urethra or bladder. Gonorrhoea and chlamydia can also be the source behind epididymitis. Common symptoms associated with epididymitis include groin pain, lump in the testicle, swollen groin area, enlarged lymph nodes and more.

Orchitis

Orchitis is an inflammation of one or both of the testicles. It can be caused by various viruses and infections such as mumps, gonorrhoea, chlamydia and more. It is also possible for men to develop orchitis along with other infections of the prostate or even epididymitis. High-risk sexual behaviours, the absence of mumps vaccination, regular urinary tract infections and long-term use of a Foley catheter can all be causes of orchitis.

Spermatocele

Another condition that presents similar symptoms to testicular cancer is spermatocele, a cyst found in the scrotal sac. The cyst consists of sperm and fluid and can appear alone or in a group. These cysts are generally harmless unless they grow large enough to require surgery or become painful. Causes for spermatocele include trauma, prior vasectomy and epididymis, amongst others.

Testicular torsion

While this condition is more frequent during infancy or puberty, some men are predisposed for testicular torsion. Testicular torsion is caused by the twisting of the spermatic cord; once twisted, the blood supply flowing to the testicle is cut, causing severe pain in the groin area. Other symptoms that can be associated with testicular torsion include a lump, blood in the semen and scrotal swelling.

Varicocele

A varicocele presents itself as swelling and widening of the veins – it is very similar to varicose veins, but varicoceles are located in the scrotal region. Sudden varicoceles can also be related to kidney tumours, so these are certainly not to be taken lightly. Symptoms associated with varicoceles include testicle lump, swelling and enlarged veins. It is also possible that a varicocele occurs without any symptoms.

Staging of testicular cancer

The idea of stages has been explored previously, but much more can be said about the various stages of testicular cancer and what they entail. In order for a physician to make a final diagnosis, staging is necessary; depending on the severity and stages of cancer, the treatment options will vary. It is also essential for you, as the patient, to truly be aware of the particular stages of your cancer.

'Testicular cancer is staged using the TNM Staging System.'

Testicular cancer is staged using the TNM Staging System, which has been developed by the American Joint Committee of Cancer. The TNM Staging System helps stage the cancer using information related to the size, location and any other relevant information about a tumour. Again, determining the precise stage of a cancer will help determine a more accurate treatment plan to attack the cancer.

The TNM Staging System uses letters to identify the characteristics of a tumour.

T stands for Tumour. This classification will be used in relation to the size of the primary tumour. Here are the various T classifications:

- T0 – no evidence of cancer

- Tis – Testicular cancer in situ; cancer cells are confined to the testicle.

- T1 – the cancer has spread to the testicular membrane.

- T2 – the cancer has spread to the lymph nodes or blood vessels of the vesicle.

- T3 – the cancer has spread to the spermatic cord.

- T4 – the cancer has spread to the scrotum.

N stands for Lymph Nodes and indicates whether or not the cancer cells have spread to the lymph nodes. Here are the various N classifications:

- N0 – no cancer cells in the lymph nodes.
- N1 – the lymph nodes are no larger than 2cm in diameter.
- N2 – At least one of the lymph nodes exceeds 2cm but is no larger than 5cm.
- N3 – At least one of the lymph nodes exceeds 5cm.

M stands for Metastasis and indicates whether or not the cancer has spread to other organs. Here are the various M classifications:

- M0 – no cancer cells found in other organs.
- M1 – cancer cells have spread to other organs.
- M1a – cancer cells spreading to the lungs or lymph nodes beyond the abdomen.
- M1b – cancer cells spreading to distant organs (liver or brain, for example).

S stands for Serum and gives more indication related to the cancer marker levels. Here are the various S classifications:

- S0 – the marker levels are normal.
- S1 – the marker levels are slightly higher than normal.
- S2 – the marker levels have moderately increased.
- S3 – the marker levels are high.

By compiling all the information related to the tumour, lymph nodes, metastasis and serum, doctors are able to accurately stage the cancer and know exactly the extent of the condition. Using all this information, it is possible to determine whether the cancer is in Stage I, II or III, along with any sub-stages.

Stage I testicular cancer

This stage indicates that the cancer is confined to the testicles and has not yet spread to other organs or lymph nodes. There are three types of Stage I testicular cancer:

'By compiling all the information related to the tumour, lymph nodes, metastasis and serum, doctors are able to accurately stage the cancer and know exactly the extent of the condition.'

- Stage IA – absence of cancer cells in testicular blood vessels.

- Stage IB – presence of cancer cells in testicular blood vessels.

- Stage IS – increase in serum marker levels after radical orchiectomy.

Stage II testicular cancer

At this stage, the cancer has spread to the lymph nodes surrounding the testicular region. There are three types of Stage II testicular cancer:

- Stage IIA.

- Stage IIB.

- Stage IIC.

All three sub-stages indicate increasing sizes of lymph nodes in the abdomen or pelvis.

Stage III testicular cancer

The third stage of testicular cancer means that cancer cells have spread beyond the groin and abdomen; cancer cells can now be found in lymph nodes of the chest, lungs or even the liver or brain. There are three types of Stage III testicular cancer:

- Stage IIIA.

- Stage IIIB.

- Stage IIIC.

Stage III can also be used to designate high levels of markers

Getting a final diagnosis

Once your doctor has explored differential diagnosis and staged your cancer, if you are indeed considered a cancer patient after all test results are in, he or she will be able to pose a final diagnosis. The final diagnosis will be deemed the most accurate diagnosis, as your doctor has most likely explored other possible causes for your symptoms, has conducted various tests and has now enough evidence to stage your condition. So, now that your diagnosis is a certainty, what should you do?

The best advice that can be given to a newly diagnosed cancer patient is to gather as much information on your condition as possible. Educate yourself, do some research on your condition, ask questions, etc. Taking an active role in your cancer care and treatment will help you understand the process and be more equipped to fight your cancer. There are many online and offline resources that you can use to learn more about your condition and understand your treatment options; you can refer yourself to the help list section of this book to get started.

In the case of testicular cancer, it is also important to think about fertility. If you are thinking of starting your own family someday or expand your existing family, you should know what your options are. While undergoing treatment for testicular cancer does not automatically mean that you'll become infertile, you should know what your options are and the possible consequences of treatment on your fertility. Ask your doctor about sperm banking or any other ways of preserving your fertility. Sperm banking is a very common practice for testicular cancer patients; while you may or may not need sperm samples due to fertility issues after treatment, you'll at least have peace of mind and will not be jeopardising your chances of having a family in the future.

Finally, stay calm. Testicular cancer is highly curable and you certainly aren't the only one affected by this condition. You can join a support group, interact with other cancer patients or read about survival stories online. Getting in touch with other individuals in your situation can help you relax and lessen your worries and concerns.

'The best advice that can be given to a newly diagnosed cancer patient is to gather as much information on your condition as possible.'

Summing Up

※ Differential diagnosis is used to consider all the possible causes of a set of symptoms.

※ While testicular cancer's main symptom is a lump on a testicle, many other conditions can present similar symptoms.

※ Common differentials associated with testicular cancer include benign tumours, epididymitis, orchitis, spermatoceles, testicular torsion and varicoceles.

※ After all differentials have been considered and testicular cancer is diagnosed, the cancer needs to be staged.

※ Testicular cancer is staged using the TNM Staging System. T stands for Tumour, N for Lymph Nodes, M for Metastasis. A fourth initial is used to represent Serum marker levels, S.

※ There are three main stages, each including three sub-stages.

※ Once you receive your final diagnosis, try to remain calm and gather as much information about your condition as possible in order to be educated and informed throughout the process. It is also recommended to join support groups and get in touch with other individuals in the same situation.

※ Testicular cancer patients are also encouraged to think about preserving their fertility, in the event that treatment will affect fertility. Sperm banking is often recommended as a preventative measure.

Chapter Five

Treatment Options

As we have mentioned several times, testicular cancer is highly curable. This is very good news for many men around the world who may receive this diagnosis at some point in their lives. There are many different treatment options available to testicular cancer patients; while some are considered invasive, there are also various non-invasive treatment options, which will be discussed in this chapter.

Your treatment options

In the end, it is important to realise that you don't always have the choice of which treatment option you can choose. Ultimately, your treatment plan will depend on different factors, including the nature of your cancer (seminoma or non-seminoma) and the stage of your cancer.

The first treatment option recommended for all types of cancer is surgery, which is considered to be an invasive procedure. By removing the cancerous testicle, or both, most of the cancer is eliminated from the body, if not all. Once the testicle is removed, other courses of treatment may be recommended, which are considered non-invasive treatment options. Such procedures can include chemotherapy or radiotherapy, for example.

Because there are a few different options, you'll probably want to do a bit of research before discussing them with your doctor. Learning about the different treatment options as well as which treatment plans are recommended for various stages of cancer can help you understand what will happen during treatment, how your body will react, how efficient each treatment option is, etc.

'There are many different treatment options available to testicular cancer patients.'

Treatment options by stage

It is essential to remember that all testicular cancers will be first attacked with surgery; while some men have the whole testicle removed, others can get away with removing only the cancerous part – however this is not common.

For Stage I testicular cancer, the surgical procedure should be enough. In the case where your cancer is seminoma, your doctor might recommend radiotherapy or chemotherapy after the testicle is removed.

Chemotherapy or radiotherapy can also be used to treat Stage IIA seminoma testicular cancer. However, for Stage IIB and IIC, only chemotherapy is usually recommended. For Stage II non-seminoma testicular tumours, chemotherapy is the most common treatment option.

All Stage III testicular cancer cases are treated with chemotherapy; however, it is possible certain lymph nodes will need to be removed with further surgical procedures.

Cancer survivors whose cancer comes back will most likely undergo rounds of chemotherapy.

> 'All testicular cancers will be first attacked with surgery.'

Radiation therapy

Radiation therapy, or radiotherapy, uses beams of radiation to destroy cancerous cells that might have been left behind after the surgical procedure. Those leftover cancer cells can spread in the body, attacking lymph nodes and organs, so undergoing radiotherapy is a way to ensure that the entire cancer is eliminated. Radiotherapy is also used as a preventive measure after surgery, to help prevent the cancer from returning.

Radiation therapy treatments for testicular cancer are usually executed 5 days a week for a month.

Because the high-energy radiation can end up killing normal cells in the process, there are certain side effects associated with radiotherapy. These can include nausea, fatigue and diarrhoea. Furthermore, it is possible to experience redness or soreness of the skin. This treatment may also affect sperm production.

Chemotherapy

Chemotherapy is defined by the intravenous administration or ingestion of anti-cancer drugs. These drugs are designed to kill the remaining cancer cells and prevent the cancer from returning, similar to radiation therapy. This particularly treatment is more often associated with non-seminoma tumours.

Chemotherapy treatments are often referred to as 'rounds'. This is because chemotherapy is administered following a cycle: the patient will receive chemotherapy on a 5-day cycle with a 2-week break between each cycle.

Side effects associated with chemotherapy present themselves under various forms, including – but not limited to:

- Nausea.
- Hair loss.
- Fatigue.
- Sore mouth.
- Temporary infertility.
- Tinnitus (ringing in the ears).
- Bruises.
- Loss of appetite.
- Numbness and tingling in the extremities.
- Shortness of breath.

On a side note, it is highly recommended not to conceive a child while receiving chemotherapy treatments or for at least a year after you've received chemotherapy treatments. The drugs used for these rounds of treatment can greatly increase the risk of birth defects in infants.

Active surveillance

For many Stage I testicular cancer patients, having the tumour removed surgically can be the only treatment option needed. Once the tumour is removed, if your cancer markers return to normal or if you do not present any indication of leftover cancerous cells and risk of relapse, your doctor may not enforce chemo or radiotherapy. Instead, you might be put on an active surveillance programme, or monitoring, in order to avoid unnecessary treatments.

If such is the case, you will be scheduled for follow-up appointments with your doctor. During these appointments, your will have CT scans, X-rays and blood work in order to monitor any trace of cancer or reappearance of symptoms. As time goes by and no signs of cancer are being noticed, your appointments will be fewer and far between. During active surveillance, it is of the utmost importance that you communicate with your doctor if you notice anything abnormal, experience any new or recurrent symptoms, or have any questions.

'During active surveillance, it is of the utmost importance that you communicate with your doctor if you notice anything abnormal, experience any new or recurrent symptoms, or have any questions.'

Research and clinical trials

In the medical field, there are always medical teams trying to come up with new treatments, new solutions and new medications to help cure diseases and health conditions. Cancer is no exception; there are hundreds of clinical trials being organised in research labs and hospitals around the world, trying to find a cure or establish a more effective course of treatment to fight cancerous cells.

In general, clinical trials can be used to test out new treatments, come up with new combinations of existing treatments, compare the various drugs already administered for treatment, or find new ways of diagnosing a condition. Clinical trials are considered to be the only way to confirm the effectiveness or non-effectiveness of a procedure.

There are two ways for a patient to take part in a clinical trial; you may be asked to be part of a trial if you present symptoms or characteristics that are idea for a particular trial, or you may research the trials available and get in touch with their administrative board. The decision remains yours; whether you are asked to take part in a trial or contact a team of your own will, if you decide not to be a part of the trial you will be respected in this decision.

In the end, taking part in a clinical trial can help find out new treatments – it can be very appealing to many to think that they might take part in developing a new cure for cancer. However, keep in mind that certain treatments are found ineffective and that it may happen that the side effects outweigh the benefits of the treatment. Clinical trials are also often restricted to very particular cases and you may or may not be eligible to participate in certain trials. Talk to your doctor to see if you are a good candidate for current research.

Surgical treatments

As mentioned earlier, all testicular cancer cases are initially treated with surgery, before moving on to non-invasive procedures such as chemotherapy or radiotherapy. There are a few different types of surgeries that can be performed to remove the tumour, and these will be explored shortly. Let's start by looking at what surgery is and what it entails.

Surgery overview

The team

Knowing that you'll have to undergo a surgical procedure can be overwhelming and, let's face it, slightly nerve-wracking. However, you should know that there will be an entire surgical team taking care of you and that each member of this team is highly trained and dedicated to offer you the very best care possible. This team includes an anaesthesiologist, surgical nurses, recovery room staff, etc. The surgical team will ensure that you are prepared prior to surgery, that everything goes smoothly during the procedure and that you are monitored and cared for after the surgery.

You'll be assigned a surgeon to perform your surgery. The particular type of surgeon will depend on your cancer, but most often than not it'll be a urologic oncologist if your cancer hasn't spread to other parts of your body. Urologic oncologists treat cancers related to the testicles, prostate, bladder and kidney; if you have an advanced stage of cancer you might require the assistance of a different specialist.

Prior to surgery

Before your surgery, you'll have to schedule a consultation and make sure that all your paperwork is in order.

During the consultation, you will meet with your assigned surgeon in order for him or her to review your medical file, perform a physical examination and establish how to perform the surgery. This is the perfect time for you to ask any questions; your surgeon must inform you of all the risks associated with the recommended procedure.

'Your surgeon must inform you of all the risks associated with the recommended procedure.'

You'll also be asked to sign consent forms stating that you agree to the procedure. Your doctor will also advise you on any restrictions, such as eating prior to surgery, smoking, drinking, supplements, etc. You'll also be advised on what to wear or bring for the procedure. You'll most likely be asked to remove all jewellery, so it is best to leave your valuables at home. Also, it is recommended to wear glasses instead of contact lenses as they are easier and quicker to remove.

Once the surgery has been agreed to and you have consented to the procedure, you'll have to undergo preoperative tests, or 'pre-ops', to prepare you for surgery. These tests may include a blood test, urine sample or scans (CT, EKG, MRI, PET, etc). All these measures are taken to ensure that your procedure goes smoothly. This way, if you need a blood transfusion or are at risk of infection or complications, the surgical team will have all the information necessary to care for you properly.

During surgery

You'll most likely be under local or general anaesthesia. Local anaesthesia means that only the region of your body that will be worked on will be numbed, while general anaesthesia means that you will be unconscious for the entire procedure.

The location of the surgery will be thoroughly disinfected and cleaned and you will most likely be shaved to reduce the risk of infection.

Radical inguinal orchiectomy

The radical inguinal orchiectomy is a surgical procedure designed to remove the cancerous testicle. The incision required for this particular procedure will be located along the beltline. This procedure can be used on both early and advanced stages of cancer and is known to be rather effective; since the entire testicle is removed, blood markers should return to normal levels after the procedure and there should be very little leftover cancerous cells.

The radical inguinal orchiectomy should not affect testosterone or fertility in the case that the remaining testicle is healthy and performs normally. It is also said that once the cancerous testicle is removed, sperm counts could improve.

In the case where both testicles are affected, a bilateral orchiectomy will be performed; this term designates the surgery used to remove both testicles. In this case, the patient will not be able to produce testosterone and sperm, and thus will be deemed infertile. Subsequently, testosterone hormone replacement may be recommended.

It is also possible for testicular cancer patients undergoing orchiectomy to request prosthetic testicles to be implanted. Your doctor can guide you as to when is the right time to perform the implantation.

'It is also possible for testicular cancer patients undergoing orchiectomy to request prosthetic testicles to be implanted.'

Retroperitoneal lymph nodes dissection (RPLND)

This particular type of surgery is used to remove the retroperitoneal lymph nodes at the back of the abdomen. RPLND is usually recommended for Stage I and IIA non-seminoma tumours. It can also be used to treat late-stage disease after rounds of chemotherapy have been completed. An incision down the middle of the abdomen will be made to remove the masses.

During retroperitoneal lymph nodes dissection, it often happens that additional cancer cells are discovered in the lymph nodes. This means that chemotherapy will most likely be necessary after the RPLND has been performed.

Temporary side effects of RPLND include bowel obstruction and infection. While the ability of having an erection and sexual intercourse should not be affected, the procedure may interfere with some nerves related to the capacity of ejaculating, thus resulting in infertility. There are other procedures designed to spare the nerves involved with ejaculation and this should be taken into consideration when establishing which procedure will be used to remove the cancer.

Retroperitoneal lymph nodes dissection may also be used to remove any residual tumours after the chemotherapy rounds have been completed. However, this procedure is more complex and will result in infertility.

Keyhole surgery

Referred to as laparoscopic retroperitoneal lymph node dissection, the keyhole surgery is a new procedure using a laparoscope to remove the lymph nodes through several cuts on the tummy.

Since this is a new procedure, not many surgeons propose this option from the outset. There are definitely benefits to the keyhole surgery, such as a faster recovery and fewer issues related to dry climax and bleeding. However, it is also essential to note that damage to the bowel, incomplete removal of the cancer and risk and relapse are associated with the keyhole surgery. Ask your surgeon about this surgery, but be advised that only experienced surgeons should perform this procedure and you should be well aware of risks before agreeing to it.

After the surgery

Recovery and aftercare are two very important parts in the success of the procedure. While individual time of recovery varies for each patient, it is important to take the necessary time to recover and rest. You may be permitted to go home soon after the operation, but depending on the type of anaesthesia received, you may be monitored for a period of time.

Local anaesthesia will allow you to recover rather quickly; most patients are sent home after a few hours, once the anaesthesia wears off. For those who were submitted to general anaesthesia, recovery will take slightly longer.

As far as aftercare goes, you must make sure to have all the information and instructions related to the steps you should take at home to ensure a successful recovery. It is recommended to walk as soon as you are able to in order to prevent clots, and enhance blood circulation throughout the body. Of course, you are encouraged to talk with your doctor to manage pain, if any, as well as to learn more about recommended nutrition or physical activity. You'll also want to make sure that someone demonstrates how or when to change your bandage if you have one.

It is also of the utmost importance to contact your doctor/surgeon should you develop redness or swelling near the incision, vomiting, fever, or anything else deemed abnormal.

Summing Up

- All types of testicular cancer will be surgically removed as a first treatment step.

- Non-invasive treatment options are used after surgery to help fight leftover cancer cells or as a preventive measure if surgery was not considered to be enough.

- Post-surgery treatment options include radiotherapy and chemotherapy.

- Active surveillance, or monitoring, may also be used for patients with a low risk of relapse in order to avoid unnecessary treatments.

- There are various clinical trials put in place to help advance research for cancer; whether a patient decides to take part or not is entirely their choice. Eligibility will be verified by the physicians running the clinical trial.

- Surgeons performing surgeries related to testicular cancer are most often urologic oncologists. Other specialists may intervene in the event of a more advanced cancer that has spread.

- A consultation is necessary prior to surgery. The consultation will allow your surgeon to determine which surgery is necessary as well as discuss all possible risks and benefits associated with the chosen procedure.

- Blood tests, urine samples and various scans may be used as preoperative tests.

- Radical inguinal orchiectomy is used to remove the entire testicle. In the event where both testicles are affected, a bilateral orchiectomy will be performed. The radical inguinal orchiectomy will most likely not affect fertility while the bilateral orchiectomy will render the patient infertile and will necessitate testosterone hormone replacement.

- Retroperitoneal lymph nodes dissection is used to remove the lymph nodes at the back of the abdomen. This procedure can be used before or after rounds of chemotherapy, depending on the stage of the cancer.

- Keyhole surgery is a new procedure used to remove the lymph nodes with a laparoscope. This procedure is said to offer a quicker recovery since the opening is not as big but rather consists of several small cuts on the tummy. Recovery and aftercare are highly important in the success of the operation.

- Your recovery time will depend on the type of anaesthesia received (local or general).

Chapter Six

General Coping and Support Advice

Of course, as with any kind of medical treatment, there are certain risks and side effects associated with each treatment option discussed thus far. While some common side effects were mentioned in the preceding chapters, it is very important to learn as much as possible about risks and side effects in order for you to make an educated decision and ask the right questions should you need to seek treatment for testicular cancer.

Coping emotionally with testicular cancer

Learning that you may have testicular cancer and preparing yourself for the battle against cancer can be life-changing. You may feel a whole range of emotions, such as overwhelmed, worried, concerned and helpless. Each man deals with and handles this news in his own way. However, there are certainly general suggestions that can be made in order to lessen your concerns and help you in the journey that awaits you.

It is very important not to be or feel alone in this difficult situation. Having a good support system, whether it be friends, family or other cancer patients is essential to ensure that you are emotionally strong and can handle the treatments, procedures and hardship that may come with the diagnosis. Don't be afraid to communicate with your loved ones and let them in on the situation. Share what you are feeling with others; your friends and family will be more than willing to stand by your side during this process and help you stay strong at this critical moment. You can also seek support and encouragement through

'Learning that you may have testicular cancer and preparing yourself for the battle against cancer can be life-changing.'

support groups and other cancer survivors; talking with other individuals who are going through the same thing, or have gone through the same thing, can be very reassuring, not to mention enlightening.

Another great suggestion for newly diagnosed testicular cancer patients is to learn as much as you can about your condition. Being informed is the best weapon against your cancer. If you know what to expect, what can happen and all the aspects of your disease, such as symptoms, treatments and more, you'll be able to fight the cancer and take care of yourself in a much more efficient way. You also need to open up to your doctor and ask questions; you'll ultimately have to make decisions when it comes to your treatment and care, and having knowledge is the only way you'll be able to make an informed decision.

Coping physically with testicular cancer

'Being informed is the best weapon against your cancer.'

Of course, while you may be emotionally shaken by the news of your diagnosis, you'll also need to prepare your body for what's to come. The cancer in itself and the treatment options offered to you will affect your body. You may experience pain and scarring after surgery; if you are undergoing chemotherapy or radiotherapy, you may feel immensely tired. Testicular cancer can also greatly affect your sex life, whether it be physically or emotionally. You may lack self-esteem or suffer from temporary infertility; do not let these temporary physical symptoms affect your moral, and keep thinking positive in order to come out of this battle victorious.

Side effects – an overview

As already mentioned, medical treatment often entails side effects, which are not always pleasant to experience. While a lot of research has been conducted as to reducing common side effects such as vomiting, nausea and pain, side effects are still a reality of medical treatments, especially the ones associated with treating cancer. Cancer greatly affects your body and so to fight back against it, aggressive treatments are needed. Most side effects only last for the duration of the treatment and will disappear shortly after surgery or rounds of chemotherapy are completed. However, you should know that other side effects may appear later on during the treatment, as opposed to right from the start, and stay for longer once the treatments have been completed. If you notice that a particular side effect is worsening, you should discuss this with your doctor. Similarly, trouble breathing, severe itching and rashes can indicate a life-threatening reaction to a particular drug or medication and measures should be taken immediately.

You should know that many side effects can be minimised or controlled with the help of your doctor. So, in the eventuality that you are affected with rather unpleasant side effects, do not hesitate to share this information with your doctor or surgeon. He or she will be able to help you get through this as smoothly as possible.

Before you start any treatment, ask your doctor about any possible side effects for your particular treatment. You should also make sure to discuss the level of care you will be needing after treatment in order to be thoroughly prepared. Treatment plans are only one step in the whole process of the battle against cancer and you should know that you might have special needs following treatment.

Side effects of surgery

As we outlined in the previous chapter, surgery is an integral part of all treatment options for testicular cancer. In this case, it is very important to know and understand the side effects of orchiectomy, as you cannot escape the procedure.

The main side effect associated with surgery is pain in the area where the surgery was conducted. However this is more than controllable and your doctor will most likely give you painkillers or other medication to help minimise any tenderness or pain in the affected region.

In the event you have both testicles removed, you will suffer from infertility and this will, unfortunately, not be a temporary occurrence. You will also need to undergo testosterone replacement therapy in order to bring your level of testosterone back to normal – testosterone is essential for a normal sex drive and to obtain an erection. Depending on how you receive hormone replacement therapy (orally, by injection or with patches) you may experience mild skin irritation.

'Many side effects can be minimised or controlled with the help of your doctor.'

If you've undergone retroperitoneal lymph node dissection, you may suffer from retrograde ejaculation. Retrograde ejaculation means that instead of coming out of the penis, semen and sperm will go back to the bladder, resulting in a dry orgasm and infertility.

Psychological side effects associated with orchiectomy can include lack of self-esteem, loss of sex drive, and various other issues. These are usually temporary and often resolve themselves once treatment is completed.

Side effects of radiation therapy

Radiation therapy has many more side effects attached to it than simple surgery. Since the radiation can affect both cancerous and normal cells, your body will be greatly affected even if normal cells usually recover from the radiation. Because there are many possible side effects associated with radiation therapy, it can be rather impossible to predict how a person will react to the treatment and you may find, when talking with other patients, that your side effects are very different from theirs. You should also know that most of these side effects are only temporary and will gradually disappear after treatment. However, late side effects may take longer to disappear or may even be permanent. Here is a general list of the most common side effects associated with radiation therapy:

Fatigue

Receiving radiation therapy treatments can make you feel very tired and interfere with your daily activities, such as simply going to work or even enjoying a day with friends and family. There are, however, things you can do to minimise the fatigue related to the radiotherapy sessions. First of all, make sure that you get enough rest to carry on normal activities. Take care of yourself and make sure that you follow your medication regimen; these small steps can help you handle the fatigue and overwhelming sensation of tiredness. You can also plan the more demanding activities earlier in the day, when you are still feeling awake and energised. This will allow you to wind down as you start getting more tired instead of forcing your body to keep up with the activities you want to do later in the day. Thankfully, fatigue associated with radiation therapy is a temporary side effect and will gradually disappear as you complete your treatment.

Skin irritation

Radiation therapy can be linked to skin irritation, as you are basically submitting your skin to beams of radiation. You may notice discolouration at the location of the radiation treatment; it can also happen that your skin looks swollen or blistered. Radiation therapy's effect on skin can be compared to a heavy sunburn; while you do have to wait for your skin to heal and go back to its normal appearance, there are things you can do to minimise discomfort and promote healing:

- Avoid scrubbing or rubbing your skin.
- Avoid the use of gauze or bandages; let the area breathe properly unless instructed otherwise by your doctor.
- Wear loose clothing as much as possible, as tight clothing may further irritate the skin.
- Do not lay in the sun or, if you do, protect the treated area by covering it with clothing.

Similarly to fatigue, skin irritation is only temporary and should improve on its own as the treatment is completed. However, it is recommended that you minimise sun exposure to the affected area for up to a year after completion of radiation therapy treatment.

'Thankfully, fatigue associated with radiation therapy is a temporary side effect and will gradually disappear as you complete your treatment.'

Hair loss

Hair loss can occur, however this is a rare occurrence when radiation therapy is used to treat testicular cancer. Hair loss following radiation therapy will most likely be experienced at the particular treated area, so unless you are having radiotherapy close to your head in the event that cancerous cells have spread, this side effect should be minimal, if at all present.

Loss of appetite

If you are undergoing radiotherapy treatments anywhere near your digestive system, you may experience a loss of appetite. However, health professionals recommend that you eat as usual in order to maintain your energy levels high enough.

Mouth discomfort

Radiotherapy could produce side effects such as mouth sores, changes in saliva production, difficulty swallowing, and more. If you experience such symptoms, talk to your doctor, as there may be ways to minimise the discomfort caused by these undesirable side effects.

Sexual difficulties

This is especially common when radiation therapy is used to treat testicular cancer. Treatment can affect sperm count or functionality of the sperm. Patients may also experience a loss of interest in sexual activity. These side effects should gradually improve in the few weeks following the completion of treatment.

Others

Other various side effects associated with radiotherapy can include hearing problems, nausea and diarrhoea. It is important to remember that radiotherapy's side effects are highly localised. For example, someone undergoing radiotherapy treatments in the groin area will most likely not lose hair or have any mouth issues. However, as it has been mentioned previously, side effects are unpredictable and differ from one patient to the other. Talk to your doctor if you experience any unusual side effects or if your side effects worsen during treatment.

Side effects of chemotherapy

Similar to radiation therapy, chemotherapy also causes a wide variety of side effects that may vary from one patient to another. The main reason behind this fact is that, just like radiation therapy, chemotherapy affects cancerous cells and normal cells, including rapidly growing cells such as hair and gums, for example. Of course, most if not all of these side effects are only temporary and will improve after completion of the rounds. The side effects associated with radiotherapy can also be observed in patients undergoing chemotherapy, with the addition of a few particular ones detailed below. Besides the well-known hair loss associated with chemotherapy, other side effects can include:

- Increased risk of infections – Because chemotherapy can lower your white blood cell count, you may be more at risk of developing infections. In order to stay as healthy as possible during treatment, you should pay special attention to basic hygiene such as washing your hands often, avoiding biting your nails and use lotion to prevent dry skin.

- Nausea and vomiting – This is a very common side effect of chemotherapy; depending on which chemotherapy drug you receive during treatment. Your doctor can help you minimise the impact of nausea and vomiting during treatment; it has also been said that electro-acupuncture provides relief of nausea and vomiting.

- Mouth sores – Chemotherapy can cause mouth sores; this is why many hospitals, if not all, offer a never-ending supply of ice-poles for patients to suck on during rounds of chemotherapy. Patients are also encouraged to avoid alcohol, tobacco and any spicy or acidic foods.

- Anaemia – Just like chemotherapy can affect your count of white blood cells, red blood cells can also be affected. A reduced number of red blood cells will lead to anaemia, which in turn leads to extreme fatigue in certain cases. It is possible to minimise this side effect by receiving a blood transfusion or using particular medications. Talk to your doctor to see if exercise can help you fight fatigue and allow yourself to rely on the help of others if you are too tired for certain tasks or activities.

Summing Up

- Cancer treatments can cause various side effects. These side effects will vary from one patient to the other and are rather unpredictable.

- Side effects from cancer treatments can include both emotional and physical side effects.

- To emotionally cope with your cancer and the journey you are about to embark on, you should surround yourselves with loved ones or join a support group to get in touch with other cancer patients and survivors.

- It can also help to gather as much information about your condition as possible in order to make informed decisions and have all the necessary tools to fight the cancer.

- The main side effect associated with surgery is pain or tenderness. Some patients may also experience a loss of sexual appetite.

- Radiotherapy can cause fatigue, skin irritation, hair loss, loss of appetite, mouth discomfort and sexual difficulties, amongst other side effects.

- Chemotherapy can cause hair loss, increased risk of infections, nausea and vomiting, mouth sores and anaemia, amongst other side effects.

- Side effects are usually temporary and will improve and disappear gradually after completion of treatment. Consult your doctor if any side effect seems to linger without improving.

Chapter Seven

Prognosis Overview

By definition, a prognosis is the potential chances for a patient to recover from a disease or condition. If you are diagnosed with testicular cancer, you have very good chances of fighting the disease and recovering, so this is very good news. There are a few different aspects that can influence the prognosis of a cancer patient. These aspects include the type and location of the cancer, the stage of the cancer, its grade and the person's general health.

Based on these aspects, doctors can better establish a prognosis. However, it is important to remember that a prognosis is not a fact set in stone, but rather a prediction of the likely course of events based on a variety of information.

Classification of a prognosis

Testicular cancer patients' prognoses can be classified in different categories. The classification of the prognosis also influences the course of treatment that will be suggested to the patient. There are three different classes:

- Good prognosis.
- Intermediate prognosis.
- Poor prognosis.

As you've probably guessed, a good prognosis is ideal. Patients diagnosed with seminoma that has not spread to organs other than the lungs and present normal AFP (alpha-fetoprotein) levels in the blood are known to have a good prognosis. On the other hand, patients diagnosed with non-seminoma can only have a good prognosis if the tumour is only located in the testicle or the abdominal wall, has not spread to organs other than the lungs and only present slightly elevated tumour marker levels.

'A prognosis is the potential chances for a patient to recover from a disease or condition.'

From there, the prognosis will move on to being considered intermediate or poor depending on how far the cancer has spread and how the tumour markers are presenting themselves. However, it is important to remember that when it comes to testicular cancer, even patients with a poor prognosis still have good chances of survival, as about 50% can be cured with somewhat aggressive treatment.

Survival rates

As previously mentioned, even testicular cancer patients with a poor prognosis still have very good chances of fighting the disease and leading healthy lives post-treatment. Survival rates are then considered impressively good.

In short, survival rates are the percentage of individuals sharing a particular type of disease who successfully survive for a certain time after the original diagnosis has been established. More often than not, statistics for survival rates will refer to the number of survivors who are still alive 5 years after the diagnosis; this includes patients who are undergoing treatment, present little or no signs or symptoms of the disease or are completely free of cancer.

'Testicular cancer in general has the very best survival rates for all types of cancer.'

However, just like the prognosis, survival rates are more of a prediction – although based on a lot of reliable information. Even if your particular condition has a very good survival rate, it may happen that your case differs from the norm.

Testicular cancer in general has the very best survival rates for all types of cancer. According to Cancer Research UK, more than 95% of men diagnosed with Stage I seminoma and non-seminoma tumours are successfully treated, while 85 to 90% of patients diagnosed with Stage II seminoma tumours successfully overcome the cancer. Even for Stage III non-seminoma patients, the outcome still stands at more than 70% of successful cases.

Of course, it is important to remember that survival rates are merely statistics and do not mean anything more than 'you have good chances'. Statistics do not indicate which treatments had the best survival rates or how a particular treatment has affected the prognosis of a patient. Also, by the time statistics are collected and published, enough time has already passed and treatments

60

may have changed, research may have been conducted and the state of patients may have changed. Do not entirely rely on survival rates to jump to conclusions.

Case studies

An article published by Carlton Gene Brown on Medscape featured case studies related to testicular cancer patients and their prognosis. Here is an extract:

'Testicular cancer (TC) strikes men between the ages of 15 and 35. If detected early, this disease can be irradicated in virtually every patient. Unfortunately, several hundred men will die from this disease each year. Research has shown that men do not know the importance of testicular self-examination, and they are not knowledgeable about TC. Nurses should be able to discuss treatment modalities, side effect management related to those treatments, and special issues dealing with sexuality, body image perception, and infertility'.

Case Study 1

'Alex is a 27-year-old man who presented to his health-care provider with an enlarging testicular mass that had been present for 1 year. He also complained of left leg pain, as well as weakness and numbness in the left lower extremity for 6 months. For the past month, Alex has needed crutches to assist with ambulation. He noted a 20-pound weight loss over the last year. Abnormalities on physical examination were tenderness over the left iliac crest and an 8cm nontender mass in the right testes. Radiographic findings included multiple 0.5 to 2cm nodules to the lung. CT scans of the abdomen showed a mass eroding the left side of the pelvis and involving gluteal muscles and a pathologic fracture of the left femoral head. A right radical orchiectomy was performed. The patient was diagnosed with Stage III non-seminomatous testicular cancer. The patient verbalized that he never knew he was supposed to inspect his own testicles for tumours and noted he never was educated by health-care providers about testicular self-examination (TSE). Alex died approximately 2 months after the initial diagnosis'.

Case Study 2

'Ryan is a 28-year-old white male who recently noted mild, bilateral breast enlargement associated with slight breast tenderness. About 2 months ago, Ryan began to experience a dull ache and a sensation of heaviness in his right testicle. Physical examination revealed a 4cm nontender mass in the right testes. Chest X-ray and CT scan of his chest and abdomen were nonremarkable. As a child, Ryan had an undescended testicle that was repaired by surgical intervention. A right radical orchiectomy was performed. Ryan notes that he recently was educated in a college health class on the risk factors of testicular cancer and how to perform testicular self-examination. A right orchiectomy and retroperitoneal lymph node dissection (RPLND) were performed and the patient was eventually diagnosed with Stage I non-seminomatous TC. Ryan will be followed by surveillance for 1 year and has almost a 100% opportunity for complete cure'.

'Case study #1 discusses a patient with a late diagnosis of testicular cancer that resulted in a poor outcome/death. In contrast, case study #2 discusses a patient who had a successful outcome because the disease was detected early, therefore allowing treatment to be initiated in a timely manner. The patient in case study #2 was knowledgeable about testicular self-examination, which led to early detection of a lump, and possibly led to long-term survival/cure as opposed to the poor outcome of the patient in case study #1.'

As you can see through this article, prognosis and survival rates are affected by many factors and something that can seem as small as performing regular self examinations regularly can have a strong influence on the outcome of a case. Early detection of testicular cancer can greatly improve survival rates and make the whole difference between a poor outcome and successful outcome; this is exactly why self-examination procedures are promoted, as they are often associated with early detection of testicular cancer.

Summing Up

- A prognosis is the likely course of events for a particular patient. This includes the likelihood of survival and helps determine the course of treatment to be used for a particular case.

- Testicular cancer patients can have a good, intermediate or poor prognosis.

- Most testicular cancer patients who have a localised cancer that has yet to spread present a good prognosis. Depending on how far the cancer has spread and how elevated the tumour marker levels are, the prognosis will be intermediate or poor. Even patients with a poor prognosis still have excellent survival rates.

- Survival rate statistics are often compiled for a 5-year period. The statistics show the number of patients who are still living, whether undergoing treatment or not, 5 years after their diagnosis.

- Survival rates for most testicular cancer patients are generally higher than 95% for Stage I cases. Stage II patients present survival rates between 85% and 90%. Even Stage III non-seminoma patients present a survival rate of more than 70%.

- Survival rates are merely statistics and by the time they are published are often deemed inaccurate – each patient has a unique cancer and cannot be compared to millions of others.

- Case studies have demonstrated that an earlier diagnosis can greatly influence the outcome of a particular case, hence the importance of conducting self-examination on a monthly basis.

Chapter Eight

Surveillance and Aftercare

It is important to understand that once you've completed your treatment for testicular cancer, it does not stop there and you may still have a lot to deal with. Many individuals struggle with aftercare or even how to go back to leading their normal lives. However, there are many tips and lots of advice that can be given to cancer patients post-treatment and there are also many resources to be used for support.

After treatment

Once you've completed your treatment for testicular cancer, you'll want to discuss with your doctor how to care for yourself once you go home. A follow-up care plan will be established; this may include follow-up visits and examinations for a few months, or even a few years. These follow-up appointments are a great way for your doctor to monitor you and make sure that everything is back to normal and that all cancer cells have been eradicated through treatment.

However, your fight is not over. Now that your treatment has been completed you'll be back to your normal life, in a way. You won't be depending on a health-care team anymore and won't have to see your doctor as often; and many patients start to feel lonely and left to themselves. Make sure that you surround yourself with loved ones and have all the support needed from friends and family to tackle your daily activities. You want to make sure that you are not actually left to yourself and that you have people who you can talk to.

'It is important to understand that once you've completed your treatment for testicular cancer, it does not stop there and you may still have a lot to deal with.'

It can also be very challenging to go back to your family life and it may take some time for your family to not see you as a cancer patient anymore – you may find yourself treated differently by family members, which is often completely involuntary. Because your family has gotten used to taking care of you and handling various tasks around the house, you may find that you are struggling to get back into the swing of things because the dynamic has changed in your house or with your friends. However, do not let this discourage you. As already mentioned, the fight is not over.

You'll also most likely be asking yourself tons of questions such as 'what if the cancer comes back?' or even 'what are the chances that it comes back?'. Dealing with the fear of recurrence is a very common challenge for cancer survivors. This is why a special emphasis is being put on follow-up visits to your doctor. Being monitored will help you ensure that if anything happens, it'll be noticed immediately and addressed efficiently. Life after cancer treatment is certainly not easy, but it is possible and it is up to you to stay strong and surround yourself with people who can support you.

'It may take some time for your family to not see you as a cancer patient anymore – you may find yourself treated differently by family members, which is often completely involuntary.'

Long-term side effects

The common temporary side effects associated with chemotherapy and radiation therapy have been addressed previously. However, there are a few long-term side effects that have been repetitively shown in testicular cancer patients. For example, radiation therapy and chemotherapy have both been known for the possibility of developing other cancers in men that have been treated for testicular cancer. However, there is no need to be alarmed right away as this issue can be addressed when it occurs and worrying ahead of time will do no good.

There are other long-term side effects that can be attributed to cancer treatments.

Lung damage

Patients who have received the drug bleomycin as part of their chemotherapy treatment are at risk of lung damage. However, only about 5% of patients have been known to develop lung damage, while the drug has been fatal for even less than 1% of patients. Possible lung damage related to bleomycin include lung scarring, however patients with lung scarring have been known to present risk factors such as cigarette smoking, previous lung injury, impaired kidney function, amongst others. Patients are recommended to stop smoking in order to lower their risk factors and should be thoroughly examined by a doctor prior to any bleomycin treatment.

Blood vessels

Bleomycin can also be related to Raynaud's phenomenon, a condition in which the blood vessels narrow causing the skin to turn white, then blue and then red. This condition is more often noticed in men who received a combination of bleomycin and vinblastine – however this combination is rarely used nowadays and less than 10% of patients have been diagnosed with this side effect.

Kidney damage

A drug called ciplastin is known to cause kidney damage in certain patients. Researchers have found that flushing the cisplatin with at least one litre of IV fluid prior to and after treatment can help minimise the risk of kidney damage. Since ciplastin is a very important drug used to treat testicular cancer, it is not recommended to avoid this drug simply for fear of kidney damage.

Hearing

Ciplastin has also been associated with an inability to hear high-pitched sounds. Ciplastin has also been known to cause tinnitus in certain patients. However, men at risk are the ones receiving higher doses of ciplastin as well as older men or men with previous hearing problems.

Fertility issues

While the majority of fertility issues observed with testicular cancer patients resolve themselves once treatment has been completed, certain patients have experienced fertility problems for a longer period of time. This is especially true for men who had a low sperm count prior to starting chemotherapy, hence the importance of discussing sperm banking before starting any cancer treatment.

Risk of recurrence

Similar to survival rates and prognosis, the risk of recurrence varies from one individual to another. Many factors will influence whether or not a cancer survivor will need to fight cancer a second time around, such as the type of cancer, treatment used, etc.

'Similar to survival rates and prognosis, the risk of recurrence varies from one individual to another.'

If you have any concerns related to the risk of recurrence of your cancer, you should not hesitate to talk with your doctor. Ask questions and make sure that you have all the facts in hand as to what the possibilities are for your cancer to come back and what signs you should look for.

Preventing recurrence – myths

Recurrence is certainly something that worries many cancer survivors. Many individuals believe that there are things that can be done to prevent cancer from recurring. However, while the myths outlined can help you lead a healthy life, remember no one thing can keep cancer from recurring.

Using vitamins and supplements

While many individuals believe that using vitamins and supplements can help keep cancer at bay, there is currently no research supporting this theory. You should talk to your doctor prior to taking any vitamin or supplement as some research has demonstrated that supplements containing high levels of a single nutrient can unfortunately have negative effects on cancer survivors.

Diet

What you eat will not influence whether or not your cancer will recur. However, it is certainly a great idea to eat healthily and cut down on fatty and high-calorie foods. Cancer survivors are highly encouraged to follow the same diet used to prevent cancer in the first place. However, you should understand that preventing cancer and preventing recurrence are two different things, and whether or not your cancer reoccurs will not directly be linked to your diet.

Physical activity

Engaging in physical activity will not prevent cancer recurrence. However, exercise in any form will help you fight depression, elevate your mood and reduce undesirable side effects such as nausea and fatigue. Cancer survivors are encouraged to engage in physical activity moderately on a daily basis. Although, you should discuss with your doctor to make sure that you are ready to engage in regular workouts and will not overwork yourself and compromise your health.

Ongoing support

The reality of fighting against and surviving testicular cancer, or any cancer for that matter, is that you'll want to make sure that you can get ongoing support when you need it most. You need to be prepared for many aspects of life with cancer and that's why it is highly recommended to surround yourself with trusted and helpful individuals, both in your health-care team and personal life.

'The reality of fighting against and surviving testicular cancer is that you'll want to make sure that you can get ongoing support when you need it most.'

Once treatment is over, you'll have to face the fact that you will live with uncertainty for years to come. You'll always wonder if a simple bruise is a symptom of something bigger, if an ingrown hair will develop into a tumour and you'll be even more concerned every time a loved one becomes sick. However, there are a few things that you can do to help you cope with this uncertainty.

For example, make sure to attend all of your follow-up visits. There is no better way to confirm that you are in good health and that you are progressing as you should than to show up for your appointments. These are an integral part of your recovery and should not be overlooked under any circumstances. While these can make you uncomfortable and leave you feeling concerned at first, you'll soon realise that every time you leave the doctor's office with good news you'll be filled with an immense sense of relief that makes the whole process worth the effort. You can also learn to celebrate your anniversary events. While this may seem gloomy at first, celebrating each year that passes after your last treatment can help you realise that you are doing great and that things are not as bad as they might seem on some days. Other things you can do to help deal with fear and uncertainty include:

- Let go of control. You do not have control over certain aspects of your cancer.

- Don't be afraid to talk with a trusted friend if you are feeling overwhelmed.

- Live in the present; this will also help you let go of the feeling of helplessness.

- Be physically active.

- Focus on the positive aspects of your life rather than focusing on the cancer.

- Take time for yourself to relax and enjoy your life.

In short, there is no better way to cope with uncertainty than to stay positive and acknowledge life's little victories and pleasures.

Cancer survivors are also encouraged to join support groups – whether online or in person – in order to interact with individuals who are going through the same thing and can better relate to them. Counselling can also help pull you through if you're having a hard time coping with life after treatment.

'Counselling can help pull you through if you're having a hard time coping with life after treatment.'

Summing Up

- Surveillance and aftercare is just as important as the treatment itself. It is necessary to ensure that you are thoroughly monitored through follow-up appointments and that you are following the instructions of your doctor once you are sent back home after treatment.

- Going back to 'normal' can be a challenge as you may still be involuntarily perceived as a cancer patient by your loved ones.

- You may experience long-term side effects of treatments. The most common ones are associated with particular chemotherapy drugs and include lung and kidney damage, hearing impairment and more.

- All testicular cancer patients are at risk of recurrence. Nothing can be done to prevent recurrence of cancer, but keeping contact with your doctor and making sure that you're living as healthily as possible can help you stay positive and informed, as well as putting all the chances on your side.

- Support is very important for cancer survivors. After treatment, cancer patients are encouraged to keep attending their follow-up appointments, celebrate anniversary events with pride and surround themselves with individuals with whom they can share their fears and talk about what they are going through.

- Cancer survivors are also highly encouraged to join support groups or seek therapy and counselling should they feel the need to talk, share their experience or learn more about other patients' stories.

Chapter Nine

Lowering the Risks
of Cancer

While nothing can prevent cancer from reccurring there are a few things that you can do to maximise your chances of not getting cancer in the first place. However, even if you do everything right, you might still end up with a testicular cancer diagnosis; keep in mind that risk factors are not the only determinant in being diagnosed with testicular cancer and that there is truly no proven way to prevent this disease.

We have already explored the known risk factors in preceding chapters – if you fall within those groups you already know that you may have bigger chances of developing testicular cancer at some point in your life. However, it is not because you do not seemingly belong in any of those classified groups that you are out of danger. Make sure that you perform regular self-examinations and take note of any changes in your testicles. While this does not lower the risks of cancer per se, it can still help you get an early diagnosis should anything abnormal present itself. Make sure that you follow the healthiest lifestyle possible; avoid overconsumption of alcohol, drugs or tobacco and make sure that you do regular exercise sessions and workouts. Good nutrition is also beneficial. Again, while this may not directly influence your chances of getting testicular cancer, staying healthy is recommended for all and can help you build a better immune system.

'Make sure that you follow the healthiest lifestyle possible.'

Raising awareness of testicular cancer

One of the main issues with testicular cancer is that even with the many campaigns and support groups available for patients, the majority of the population is still not thoroughly informed on the topic. Many men are not aware that self-examinations are recommended, and even doctors omit to mention to risk patients that they might want to look for anything abnormal since they belong in the increased risk factor groups.

Raising awareness of testicular cancer is a very important matter; when the greater public are more knowledgeable about the issue at hand, the survival rates of patients will increase even higher as more cancers will be diagnosed early, rather than late.

Research related to testicular cancer

There are a few research projects on the go related to testicular cancer. While great progress has been made throughout the last few decades, there is always room for improvement. However, it is certainly interesting to note that back in the 1960s, only a low 6% of testicular cancer patients survived; this certainly puts into perspective the advancement and discoveries made in relation to this particular disease. One of the main reasons behind this spectacular progress is the development of carboplatin and cisplatin, which have both become standard treatments for testicular cancer.

As far as new research goes, some researchers have been investigating gene variations that could lead to increased risk factors – however this is still under investigation.

Doctors are also trying to understand how they can predict reoccurrence of cancer and subsequently base the amount of therapy necessary on this fact in order to ensure that all men receive the most appropriate treatment after diagnosis.

Of course, new drugs and new drug combinations are always being tested in order to keep the advancement going as far as discovering new cures and treatments is concerned. This research is often conducted under clinical trials,

Support groups

As you will discover in the help list of this book, there are many support groups dedicated to providing help and support to testicular cancer patients and testicular cancer survivors. Some of these support groups include:

- Everyman Support Group.
- Patient UK.
- Maggie's Centre.
- Mind Over Matter.

You are strongly encouraged to inquire about these groups and get in touch with associations that can provide the level of support and encouragement needed to pull through this challenge. Sharing your own story and discovering how others coped can give you an entirely new perspective on your battle with cancer and your life in general.

Testicular cancer campaigns

As mentioned previously, raising awareness of testicular cancer is one of the many steps that can be taken to increase the number of early diagnoses and minimise late diagnosis, which can be fatal. Around the world, there are various campaigns in motion such as the following:

- Everyman UK – Everyman UK is constantly looking for volunteers to get involved in events and awareness campaigns. Everyman UK works year-round to help raise awareness and everyone is encouraged to get involved through the many roles offered.

- Blue September – This is an Australian campaign aimed at raising nationwide awareness of men-specific cancers (including testicular cancer of course), as well as fundraising for the cause. All funds raised through Blue September are sent to the Australian Research Foundation and Bowel Cancer Australia.

- Check Yo Nutz – Based in the USA, this campaign has been put in place to raise awareness of testicular cancer. It was originally started by the Canisius

'Raising awareness of testicular cancer is one of the many steps that can be taken to increase the number of early diagnoses and minimise late diagnosis, which can be fatal.'

College in Western New York along with the Roswell Park Cancer Institute. Check Yo Nutz promotes self-examination procedures for men between 15 and 40 years old.

If you are a testicular cancer survivor or know someone who is battling with the condition, do not hesitate to contact awareness groups in your area to take part in those campaigns. The only way these organisations can keep up the good work they are currently doing is through the hard work and support of volunteers, as well as donations. Getting involved is a great way to show your support for the cause and can go a long way in helping raise awareness, fundraise for research and more. Donating a few pounds or sparing a few hours of your time can go a long way.

Summing Up

- While there is no real way to prevent testicular cancer in the first place, or lower risks of developing the cancer, men are encouraged to maintain a healthy lifestyle and keep themselves updated on the increased risk factors that have been associated with the condition. Men who fall under the risk factor categories should be especially vigilant with their health and carry out regular self-examinations.

- Raising awareness of testicular cancer is a great way to diffuse information related to the condition, as well as promote self-examination and raise funds for the cause.

- Research is always on the go when it comes to testicular cancer. New drugs and drug combinations, as well as ways to predict cancer reoccurrence are some of the main concerns being investigated in research.

- There are awareness campaigns being put in place around the world; the groups leading those campaigns are always looking for volunteers.

Glossary

Aftercare

Care needed after a treatment or surgery; can also refer to the support needed for a patient to make the transition back into normal life and daily activities.

Anaemia

A condition defined by a deficiency of red blood cells. Symptoms can include a lack of energy and vitality, paleness of the skin and shortness of breath.

Anaesthesia

Artificial numbness or local insensibility. This is induced by doctors in order to perform surgery or other painful procedures.

Clinical trial

Research including the investigation of a new treatment showing promising results but that remains untested on humans. Clinical trials are used to develop data and statistics related to the efficiency of a particular new or improved treatment.

Cryptorchidism

A particular medical condition presented when one or both testicles do not descend to their usual position. Undescended testes are usually unable to function.

Diagnosis

The process in which a doctor or a team of doctors can determine the cause of a set of symptoms; coming to a diagnosis usually involves thorough examination and tests.

Differential diagnosis

The process in which a doctor or a team of doctors can determine the multiple causes or related causes to a particular set of symptoms. Differential diagnosis can help come up with a final diagnosis by exploring all possible avenues or options.

Germ cell tumour

A particular type of cancer that has developed in the ovary or testes. The most common type of testicular cancer.

Laparoscopy

The exploration of a body cavity using a laparoscope. The laparoscope is a small tube that can be inserted through the abdomen, allowing the doctor to see the internal organs.

Lump

A mass, or bump, found under the skin.

Metastasis

The transference, or spreading, of malignant or cancerous cells. The spreading occurs through the blood, lymphatic vessels or membranous surfaces.

Mouth sores

Ulcer located inside the mouth. These oral lesions can make it difficult to eat and talk.

Oncologist

A doctor specialised in treating cancer – the science studying cancer is called oncology.

Orchiectomy

A surgical procedure in which one or both of the testicles are removed.

Pathologist

Specialist in pathology. Pathology is the branch of medicine focusing on determining the cause and origin of diseases.

Prognosis

Classification used to determine how positive or negative the possible outcome of a disease is. Cancer patients usually receive one of three prognoses: good, intermediate or poor, depending on the status of their cancer.

Recovery

Return to a healthy state; the fight against cancer, if successful, results in 'recovery'. The word recovery can also be used to describe the process of getting better and healing.

Relapse

When a disease that has been treated comes back, it can be defined as a relapse. The reoccurrence of cancer is a relapse.

Remission
Remission is the period of time when symptoms of the cancer reduce or disappear following treatment.

Side effects
Undesirable symptoms caused by certain drugs or treatments used to cure or heal a disease or condition.

Staging
The act of determining the particular stage of a cancer. Cancer can be classified in various stages according to how much it has spread and which organs it has spread to.

Stromal tumour
A tumour arising in the connective tissue of an organ.

Testicles/testes
The part of the male reproductive system that produce sperm situated in a sac underneath the penis called the scrotum.

Help List

Helplines

Cancer Aid and Listening Line (CALL)
0845 123 2329
www.canceraid.co.uk
Emotional support and home-based practical help for people living with
cancer, their carers and families.

CancerHelp UK
Freephone helpline: Freephone 0808 800 4040 (to talk to a cancer information
nurse).
www.cancerhelp.org.uk
Provides a free information service about cancer and cancer care for people
with cancer and their families.

Macmillan Cancer Support
Macmillan Cancer Support, 89 Albert Embankment, London, SE1 7UQ
Freephone helpline: 0808 808 0000 (To talk to a specialist cancer nurse to get
confidential, accurate and up-to-date information about any aspect of cancer.)
www.macmillan.org.uk
Macmillan is dedicated to supporting people affected by cancer. Macmillan
develops and provides a wide range of medical, practical, emotional and
financial services, including the distribution of information. Recognised as the
UK's leading source of high-quality information on every cancer.

Tenovus Cancer Information Centre (Wales)

Helpline: 0808 808 1010
www.tenovus.org.uk

The Ulster Cancer Foundation (Northern Ireland)

Freephone helpline: 0800 783 3339
www.ulstercancer.org
Providing information, counselling, and support.

Support Groups and Forums

Everyman Support Group

Tel: 01727 730652 / 020 7153 5375
Email: everyman@icr.ac.uk
Wendy Gough, Everyman supporter, lost her son to testicular cancer.
She has set up the Everyman Support Group which offers help, advice and
awareness talks on prostate, testicular and breast cancer.

Maggie's Centres

Maggie's Centres, 1st Floor, One Waterloo Street, Glasgow, G2 6AY
Tel: 0300 123 1801
Email: enquiries@maggiescentres.org
www.maggiescentres.org
Maggie's is about empowering people to live with, through and beyond cancer
by bringing together professional help, communities of support and building
design to create exceptional centres for cancer care.
Maggie's Centres are for anyone affected by cancer. They are places where
people are welcome whenever they need us – from just being diagnosed,
or undergoing treatment, to post-treatment, recurrence, end of life or in
bereavement.

Mind Over Matter

14 Blighmont Crescent, Millbrook, Southampton, Hampshire, SO15 8RH
Tel: 01703 775611
A voluntary group set up to increase men's awareness of testicular cancer.
Offers mutual support and self-help for men with testicular cancer through
befriending.

Cancer Information Resources

Cancer Research UK Information and Support

Angel Building, 407 St John Street, London, EC1V 4AD
Tel: 020 7242 0200
www.cancerresearchuk.org
Cancer Research UK is the largest cancer research organisation in the world,
outside the USA. We are the European leader in the development of new anti-
cancer drugs. We fund research on all aspects of the disease from its causes,
to treatment and prevention, education and psychological support for patients.

Cancer Support Scotland

Tel: 0141 211 0122
Shelley Court, Gartnavel Complex, Glasgow, G12 0YN
www.cancersupportscotland.org
A Scottish charity here to support people affected by cancer. The charity has
its main centre at Gartnavel Hospital, Glasgow, and has a number of support
groups covering Scotland.
Cancer Support Scotland, formally known as Tak Tent, offers one-to-one talking
therapy (counselling) and complementary therapies to people affected by
cancer, including family and friends, before, during and after treatment.
This charity also brings people together in community support groups to
discuss their feelings and anxieties when faced with a cancer diagnosis.
Services are offered free of charge and rely on donations and legacies from
the public to allow us to continue to support the people who need it most.

Healthtalkonline

www.healthtalkonline.org

Healthtalkonline is the award-winning website of the DIPEx charity. Healthtalkonline and its sister website, Youthhealthtalk, let you share in more than 2,000 people's experiences of over 60 health-related conditions and illnesses. You can watch videos or listen to audio clips of the interviews, read about people's experiences if you prefer and find reliable information about specific conditions, treatment choices and support.

Irish Cancer Society

Cancer helpline: 1 800 200 700

www.cancer.ie

We are Ireland's national cancer charity. We listen, we support, we provide care, we create awareness, we provide information, we fund research and we influence decisions about cancer. We are with you on every step of your cancer journey.

The Mark Gorry Foundation

www.themarkgorryfoundation.co.uk

The Mark Gorry Foundation, a testicular cancer charity, was set up by Mark Gorry during his fierce battle with testicular cancer in 2009. Throughout all the emotion, the turmoil and the symptoms, Mark began to generate an idea of setting up a foundation to support those who helped him through his illness; a foundation that would positively impact the treatment of cancer in the future as well as work at raising awareness amongst young men of the symptoms of testicular cancer. Due to the late detection of his disease, Mark's personal goal was to start a movement which encouraged men to 'stay on the ball'; he wanted other men to be informed of testicular cancer symptoms, promoting early detection.

NHS Choices

www.nhs.uk

NHS Choices is the online 'front door' to the NHS. It is the country's biggest health website and gives all the information you need to make choices about your health.

Orchid

Orchid, St Bartholomew's Hospital, London, EC1A 7BE
Tel: 0203 465 5766
www.orchid-cancer.org.uk
Orchid exists to save men's lives from testicular, prostate and penile cancers through a range of support services, pioneering research and promoting awareness. Over 37,400 men will be diagnosed with a male-specific cancer in 2012; from sons to grandfathers, all men face the risk of prostate, penile or testicular cancer. Orchid plays a leading role in the fight against male cancer through world class research, awareness and education campaigns and by supporting patients.

Testicular Cancer Awareness (Scotland)

Tel: 01875 341158
www.freewebs.com/tcas
We aim to offer support to anyone who has been diagnosed with testicular cancer, their families, carers and friends. Our support service gives people the chance to get in touch with someone who has been through testicular cancer, either as a patient, relative (including, spouse, parent) or carer.

The Ulster Cancer Foundation (Northern Ireland)

40-44 Eglantine Avenue, Belfast, BT9 6DX
Tel: 00 44 +28 9066 3281
www.ulstercancer.org
Providing information, counselling and support. Patient-to-patient home and hospital visits are available. Support services for patients include art therapy and a resource centre. Support groups are also available for different types of cancer throughout the province. Professional counsellors available for patients and their families in the cancer centre and each of the cancer units. Resource and information centre is available.

References

American Cancer Society. Available at http://www.cancer.org/ Accessed on 3 March 2012.

American Society of Clinical Oncology. Available at http://www.cancer.net Accessed on 5th April 2012.

Armenian Medical Network. Available at http://www.health.am Accessed on 4th April 2012.

BBC, Doctors' Testicular Checks Warning, 13 May 2002. Available at http://news.bbc.co.uk/1/hi/health/1977504.stm Accessed on 4th April 2012.

BestHealth. Available at http://www.besthealth.bmj.com Accessed on 4th April 2012.

Brown, Carlton Gene, MSN, RN, AOCN, Medscape Today, 21 April 2004. Available at http://www.medscape.com/viewarticle/473629 Accessed on 5th April 2012.

Canadian Cancer Society. Available at http://www.cancer.ca Accessed on 5th April 2012.

Cancer.net. Available at http://www.cancer.net Accessed on 4th April 2012.

Cancer Research UK, About Testicular Cancer: A Quick Guide. Available at http://cancerhelp.cancerresearchuk.org/prod_consump/groups/cr_common/@cah/@gen/documents/generalcontent/about-testicular-cancer.pdf Accessed on 4th April 2012.

eHealthMD. Available at http://ehealthmd.com/content/what-testicular-cancer Accessed on 3 March 2012.

Everyday Health. Available at http://www.everydayhealth.com Accessed on 5th April 2012.

Graham, Tim; The Ignorance and Fear of Testicular Cancer, 6th April 2011. Available at http://espn.go.com/blog/afceast/post/_/id/27692/the-ignorance-and-fear-of-testicular-cancer Accessed on 5th April 2012.

Health24. Available at http://www.health24.com Accessed on 4th April 2012.

Kinkade, Scott; Testicular Cancer, May 1999. Available at http://www.aafp.org/afp/1999/0501/p2539.html Accessed on 5th April 2012.

Macmillan Cancer Support. Available at http://www.macmillan.org.uk Accessed on 4th April 2012.

Mayo Clinic. Available at http://www.mayoclinic.com Accessed on 5th April 2012.

MDGuidelines. Available at http://www.mdguidelines.com Accessed on 4th April 2012.

MedlinePlus. Available at http://www.nlm.nih.gov/medlineplus Accessed on 4th April 2012.

Medpedia. Available at http://www.wiki.medpedia.com Accessed on 5th April 2012.

Memorial Sloan-Kettering Cancer Center. Available at http://www.mskcc.org Accessed on 4th April 2012.

National Cancer Institute. Available at http://www.cancer.gov Accessed on 5th April 2012.

NHS Choices. Available at http://www.nhs.uk Accessed on 4th April 2012.

Oncolink. Available at http://www.es.oncolink.org Accessed on 4th April 2012.

TC-Cancer. Available at http://www.tc-cancer.com/ Accessed on 3 March 2012.

Testicular Cancer Society. Available at http://www.testicularcancersociety.org Accessed on 4th April 2012.

The Testicular Cancer Resource Center. Available at http://www.tcrc.acor.org Accessed on 4th April 2012.

WebMD – Cancer Health Center. Available at http://www.webmd.com/cancer Accessed on 5th April 2012.